The Story of
EASTER

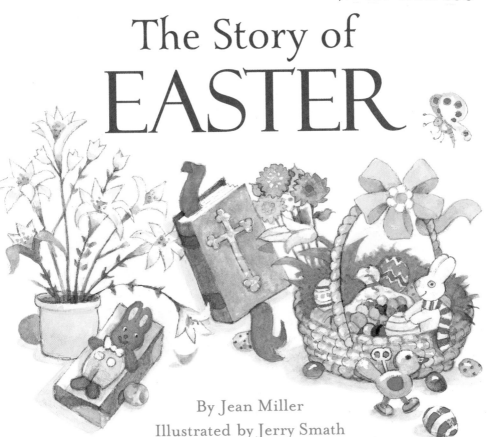

By Jean Miller

Illustrated by Jerry Smath

A GOLDEN BOOK · NEW YORK

Text copyright © 1999, 2018 by Penguin Random House LLC.
Cover art and interior illustrations copyright © 2018 by Jerry Smath.
All rights reserved. Published in the United States by Golden Books, an imprint of Random House
Children's Books, a division of Penguin Random House LLC, 1745 Broadway, New York, NY 10019,
and in Canada by Penguin Random House Canada Limited, Toronto. Originally published with
different illustrations by Golden Books Publishing Company, Inc., in 1999. Golden Books, A Golden
Book, A Little Golden Book, the G colophon, and the distinctive gold spine are registered trademarks
of Penguin Random House LLC.
rhcbooks.com
Educators and librarians, for a variety of teaching tools, visit us at
RHTeachersLibrarians.com
Library of Congress Control Number: 2016939010
ISBN 978-0-399-55514-5 (trade) — ISBN 978-0-399-55515-2 (ebook)
Printed in the United States of America
10 9 8 7 6 5 4 3 2

Long ago in a land called Judea, a man named Jesus
taught people about God's love for them.

People came from all over the land to hear what he
had to say.

But not everyone liked Jesus. Some leaders worried
that the people liked Jesus more than them. And they
didn't like what Jesus said—that he was the Son of God.

Jesus met with twelve of his closest followers, who were called disciples. "The Passover feast is in two days," he said. "We shall meet then and eat together."

A disciple named Judas heard that Jesus's enemies wanted to capture him. Judas met with them in secret. He offered to point Jesus out in return for thirty pieces of silver.

Jesus and his twelve disciples gathered together for the Passover feast. As they ate, Jesus watched them sadly. "One of you will betray me to my enemies," he said.

This upset the disciples. They stared at each other, wondering who could betray Jesus. Judas slipped out of the room as soon as he could.

Jesus asked for God's blessing on the bread, then broke it and gave it to the disciples. "Take this, for this is my body, which I am giving up for you," he said. "Take it and eat." Holding up a cup of wine, Jesus gave thanks and shared it with his disciples, saying, "This is my blood, poured out for you. Take it and drink."

After the meal, Jesus took his disciples to the Garden of Gethsemane. He asked them to come with him and keep him company while he prayed to God. But after a while, the disciples fell asleep. Jesus sadly watched their slumber. He knew he would soon be leaving them.

Suddenly, Judas arrived with a large band of men. He went up to Jesus and kissed him.

That was the signal Jesus's enemies were waiting for. They surrounded Jesus and led him away. Terrified, the disciples fled.

When Judas saw this, he regretted what he had done.

Judas tried to return the money Jesus's enemies had paid him. But it was too late.

Roman soldiers took Jesus to a place called Golgotha. There he was crucified, along with two thieves. Before he died, Jesus asked God to forgive those who had betrayed him.

A man named Joseph of Arimathea asked for permission to bury Jesus. He tenderly wrapped the body of Jesus in fine white linen and laid him in a tomb carved into a rock.

Two grieving women, Mary Magdalene and Jesus's mother, Mary, watched as Joseph closed the entrance with a large stone.

Three days passed. Mary, the mother of Jesus, and Mary Magdalene came to visit the tomb.

There they were greeted by a beautiful angel. "The tomb is empty," the angel told them. "Jesus has risen to heaven, as he said he would. You must travel to Galilee, where you will find him."

As the two women walked, they were met by Jesus. He greeted them, saying, "All hail! Tell my brother disciples to go to Galilee—they will see me there!"

Jesus met his disciples in Galilee. He spoke to them, saying, "Go among the nations and teach my words. Baptize the people in the name of the Father, Son, and Holy Spirit." And Jesus comforted them, telling them to remember that he would be with them always, until the end of the world.

These events became the Christian holiday of
Easter. The final week of Jesus's life came to be known
as Holy Week, which begins with Palm Sunday.

On that day, the Sunday before Easter, Jesus had
entered Jerusalem. People greeted him waving palm
branches. It is now a tradition for worshippers to
receive palm branches or little crosses made of palm
fronds in church on Palm Sunday.

The Passover meal that Jesus ate with his disciples took place on a day that is now called Maundy Thursday. At this meal, Jesus commanded his disciples to love one another. The meal became known as the Last Supper.

Good Friday, also called God's Friday, was the day when the Romans put Jesus on a cross.

The cross became a symbol of Christianity, and the followers of Jesus came to be called Christians. Easter falls on a Sunday because that was the day Jesus was resurrected from the dead. Jesus's ascent to heaven forty days later is called the Ascension.

Spring flowers are used to decorate churches and homes for Easter. The favorite and most beloved of Easter plants is the beautiful white Madonna lily.

Christians consider Easter their most important Holy Day. There are special church services on Easter Sunday. People wear their best clothes. Families and friends gather for a festive Easter dinner.

In many cultures, eggs are a symbol of life. This is why brightly colored eggs are an important part of Easter celebrations.

Long ago at Easter time, people put colored eggs in grass nests made to look like birds' nests. Today people decorate Easter baskets with ribbons and spring flowers and fill them with colored eggs and Easter candy.

In the country of Ukraine, women make beautifully decorated Easter eggs called Pysanky (pee-SANK-ee). The word means "written eggs."

Pysanky are often presented to relatives and friends. They are treasured gifts, kept for many years.

In England, Scotland, Ireland, and Wales, many people believe that the sun dances as it rises on Easter Sunday. People get up early in the morning and gather outdoors to wait for this to happen.

And in many places, it is an old custom to call friends and relatives on Easter morning with the greeting "Christ is risen," to be answered with "He is risen indeed!"